MAKER
KIDS

High-Tech
DIY Projects
with
Robotics

Maggie Murphy

PowerKiDS press

New York

Published in 2015 by The Rosen Publishing Group, Inc.
29 East 21st Street, New York, NY 10010

First Edition

Editors: Jennifer Way and Jacob Seifert
Book Design: Andrew Povolny
Photo Research: Katie Stryker

Photo Credits: Cover Thomas Trutschel/Photothek/Getty Images; p. 4 Christopher Halloran/Shutterstock.com; p. 5 Jay Directo/AFP/Getty Images; p. 6 Larry Burrows/The LIFE Picture Collection/Getty Images; p. 7 William West/AFP/Getty Images; p. 8 Kemal Ba?/iStock/Thinkstock; p. 9 Robert Cianflone/Hulton Archive/Getty Images; p. 10 The Washington Post/Getty Images; p. 11 c.d. stone; pp. 15, 16, 17, 20–25 Katie Stryker; p. 12 Peter Cade /Iconica/Getty Images; pp. 13, 26 Bloomberg/Getty Images; p. 14 Echo/Cultura/Getty Images; p. 18 Krystian Nawrocki/E+/Getty Images; p. 19 36clicks/iStock/Thinkstock; p. 27 Andrew Kornylak/Aurora/Getty Images; p. 28 Said Khatib/AFP/Getty Images; p. 29 Brendon Thorner/Stringer/Getty Images.

Library of Congress Cataloging-in-Publication Data

Murphy, Maggie, author.
High-tech DIY projects with robotics / by Maggie Murphy. — First edition.
    pages cm. — (Maker kids)
Includes index.
ISBN 978-1-4777-6669-9 (library binding) — ISBN 978-1-4777-6675-0 (pbk.) —
ISBN 978-1-4777-6656-9 (6-pack)
1. Robots—Design and construction—Juvenile literature. 2. Robotics—Juvenile literature. 3. LEGO Mindstorms toys—Juvenile literature. I. Title. II. Title: High-tech do-it-yourself projects with robotics.
TJ211.2.M87 2015
629.8'92—dc23
                                    2013046684

Manufactured in the United States of America

CPSIA Compliance Information: Batch #WS14PK9: For Further Information contact Rosen Publishing, New York, New York at 1-800-237-9932

Contents

Be a Robot Builder!

Robots are moving machines that are **programmed** to perform actions without human help. Robots can do small tasks to help you, such as vacuum a room. They can also do things humans cannot do safely, including explore the surface of Mars!

Scientists can send a robot called a rover to explore other planets. This is a copy of the rover *Curiosity* that is being used to explore Mars.

Kids all over the world have fun learning to build robots. You can even join a club and enter robot-building competitions.

This book will not just tell you about robots. It will also teach you how to make them! All over the world, kids like you are taking part in the maker movement. This means they are learning how to build high-tech projects themselves. Building a robot might sound difficult, but it is actually fun and very easy to do! Read on for more information and a **robotics** project with step-by-step instructions.

From the Beginning to Now

People have been thinking up and building robot-like machines for hundreds of years. For example, Leonardo da Vinci designed a robotic knight in the late 1400s. It would have been able to sit, stand, and move its arms by using a system of **pulleys** and cables. In the seventeenth century, mechanical wooden dolls called *karakuri ningyo* served tea in Japanese homes. They moved with the help of strings and **cogs**.

This is W. Grey Walter's robot Elmer. A dome was put over the top of it, which is part of the reason it was also called a tortoise robot.

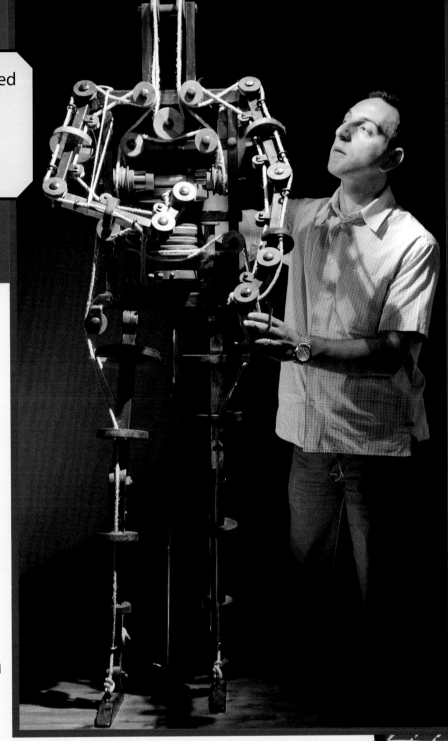

Modern researchers have used Leonardo's plans to build his robotic knight, as seen here. They found that it works as Leonardo had intended.

While early robots had to be operated, or controlled, by humans, modern robots can move and act on their own. One of the earliest robots that could do this was created in 1948 when William Grey Walter built Elmer. Elmer was a small robot that moved around by detecting light. If it bumped into something, it could change direction to move around the object. Elmer was the first robot able to interact with its environment on its own.

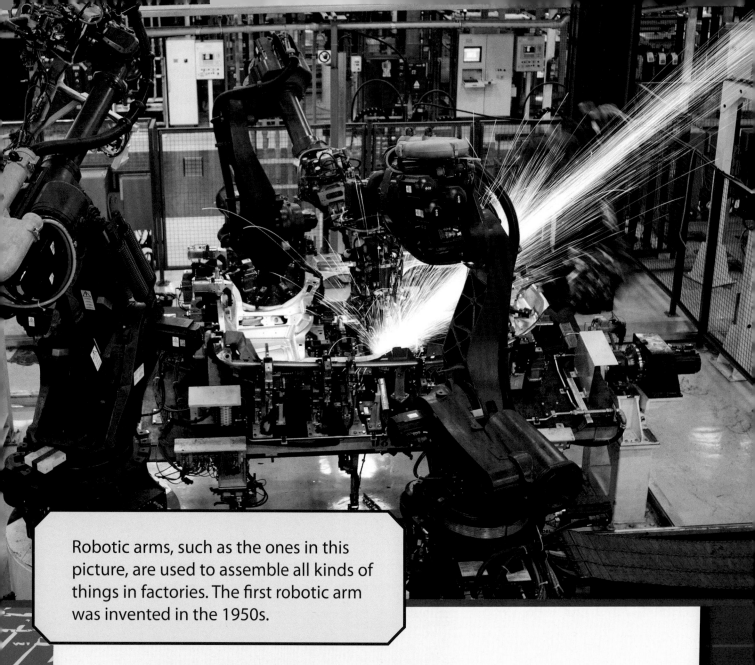

Robotic arms, such as the ones in this picture, are used to assemble all kinds of things in factories. The first robotic arm was invented in the 1950s.

Today, robots play a large part in our lives. Robots are able to perform **complex** tasks over and over again without getting bored or tired. In fact, robots often perform these tasks better and faster than humans. This means that you can find robots in most factories and warehouses. Robots can put together cars, assemble electronics such as cell phones and cameras, and package goods.

Robots often perform tasks that can be dangerous to humans. Special kinds of robots have been created to disarm bombs, search disaster sites, and explore the deep seas.

Robots are also fun. There are plenty of robotic toys to buy, and many people build their own robots. Sometimes they even build them so they can battle each other in competitions.

Famous Robots

The word "robot" comes from the Czech word *robota*, meaning "forced work." The word was first used by a Czech writer named Karel Čapek in his 1920 play *R.U.R.*, which stood for "Rossum's Universal Robots." Since then, robots have appeared in many other plays, books, movies, and television shows. Some famous **fictional**, or made-up, robots include R2-D2 and C-3PO from the Star Wars movies and WALL-E, who starred in his own movie.

These robotic dogs can walk, play, and bark. The goal of many companies that build robots is to make them as lifelike as possible.

How Do Robots Work?

Many robots are built and programmed to do specific tasks, like mowing a lawn or traveling through a sewer system. However, most robots have the same kinds of basic parts.

First, robots use **sensors** to gather information about the environment or things around them. The information a sensor gathers is called input. There are many different kinds of sensors. Some sensors detect heat, while others sense light, sound, or something else.

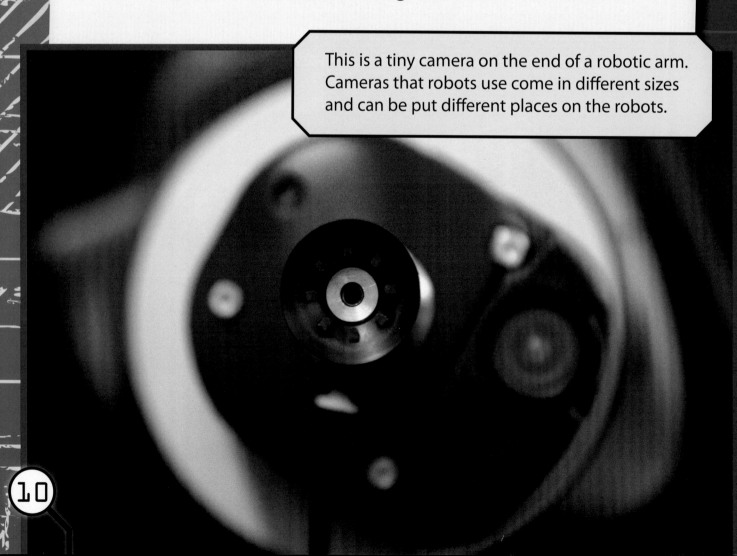

This is a tiny camera on the end of a robotic arm. Cameras that robots use come in different sizes and can be put different places on the robots.

Microcontrollers

Many robotics projects are built with microcontroller boards, like the one seen here. These are like small computers that can be programmed. The programs stored in a microcontroller board's memory help process information from sensors and then tell the robot how to act. Adafruit, Arduino™, and BeagleBone are popular microcontroller boards because they are easy to use and don't cost a lot of money.

Once a sensor has gathered input, it sends it to a computer that controls the robot. This computer is like the robot's brain. It is programmed to understand the input a sensor sends to it. It processes the input and then sends new information to other parts of the robot to make it act in a certain way.

Robots use moving parts to perform actions. Some robots have humanlike arms and hands that allow them to do complex tasks. Many robots are able to move around. Wheels and treads can help them move over the ground, and propellers can help them move through water or fly through the air. These and other actions robots do are called output.

When building a robot, it is best to decide first what you want it to do. Then you can design it to do just that.

The camera gathers input and sends it to this robot's computer. The computer tells the propellers to spin, which is output.

Finally, robots cannot work without a power source. Batteries power many robots. When the batteries run out, they need to be recharged or replaced with new ones. Some robots use alternative power sources like **solar panels**, which collect sunlight and change it into energy the robot can use.

Robotics Clubs and Teams

You can have a lot of fun working with others to build robots. One way to do this is by joining a robotics club or team.

Robotics clubs are groups that build robots, share ideas, and allow you to meet other kids who are also interested in robotics. Teams do many of the same things, but they also go to competitions. During a competition, kids on each team work together to complete different tasks.

Robotics clubs and teams have an adult expert who will help you and teach you many exciting things.

One big task of starting a robotics club or team is getting the materials you need. A teacher or adult can help you do this.

Your school might have a robotics club or team already. Lists of community clubs can be found online at Makezine.com/maker-community-groups or by going to Makerspace.com and clicking on Directory. If there is not a club or team near you, ask a teacher or other adult to help you start one! Makerspace.com offers a free PDF book with information that can help you get started.

LEGO Mindstorms

One way to get into robotics is by using a kit. Kits come with everything you need to build a specific robot. One kind of kit is the LEGO Mindstorms kit. Each comes with sensors, a computer called a Brick, motors to make your robot move, and hundreds of special LEGO pieces. This allows you to build many different robots.

Lego.com/en-us/mindstorms/downloads has free building instructions and software you can download. If you're looking for a challenge, you can design and build a robot and then write its program all on your own.

The larger piece seen here is the Brick. The smaller pieces are sensors. You connect these to the body of a LEGO Mindstorms robot to make it do things.

This robotics team uses only LEGO Mindstorms kits. They build and test robots during meetings after school and then enter them in competitions.

Robot Commander

With the EV3 Brick, you can control your LEGO Mindstorms robots like never before. If you have access to a smartphone, you can have an adult help you download LEGO Commander, a free app that lets you control your robot with your phone in real time. Just download the app, turn on the Bluetooth settings on your EV3 Brick and your smartphone, and link them together. Then tap, swipe, and tilt your smartphone to see your robot go.

One fun thing to do with a LEGO Mindstorms kit is to find out what other people are doing with theirs. Lots of people share their designs, photos, and videos of their LEGO Mindstorms projects at Lego.com/en-us/mindstorms/community.

Make a Robot from Scratch!

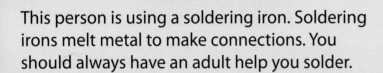

This person is using a soldering iron. Soldering irons melt metal to make connections. You should always have an adult help you solder.

There are many robotics projects you can do without having to use a kit. Many robots can be made using common tools, household materials, and a few high-tech parts.

Safety Tips

Building a robot is very fun, but it can also be dangerous. If a project requires you to glue, solder, wire, drill, or cut anything, you need to have an adult help you with those steps. You should also have an adult help you cover your wire connections with electrical tape so they do not **short-circuit**, or break. Finally, do not add the battery or power source to your robot until you have finished building and programming it.

A hardware store may not have the high-tech parts you will need for your projects, but it will have metal, screws, wires, and tools.

To find a robotics project, ask a guardian or teacher to help you search the Internet. There are tons of websites with robot-building projects for kids, including some with video **tutorials**, or lessons. Your school or library may also have books or magazines that include robotics projects.

Each project should have a list of the parts and tools you will need to build it, as well as step-by-step directions for putting it together. You can find many parts and tools you need at a local hardware or hobby store. You might need to have an adult help you order some of the high-tech parts off the Internet, though. Radioshack.com, Digikey.com, and RobotShop.com carry many parts you will need.

Mini Project: Dizzy Robot

This project is quick, fun, and will make a miniature robot that moves around on its own. You will need an adult to help you cut the tin. If the edges of the metal are sharp when you cut it, use a file to remove the sharp edges.

You will need:

- Thin crafting metal that is .008 inch (.2 mm) thick
- Button battery (LR44)
- 3VDC vibration motor
- Metal file
- Wire strippers

1

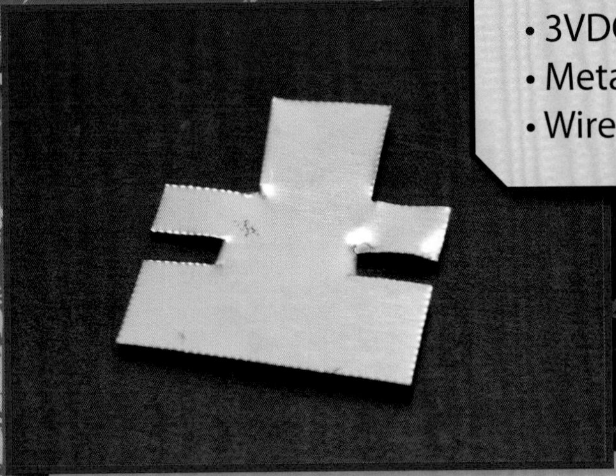

2

Cut out a 1-inch (2.5 cm) square of crafting metal. Cut it into the shape seen above.

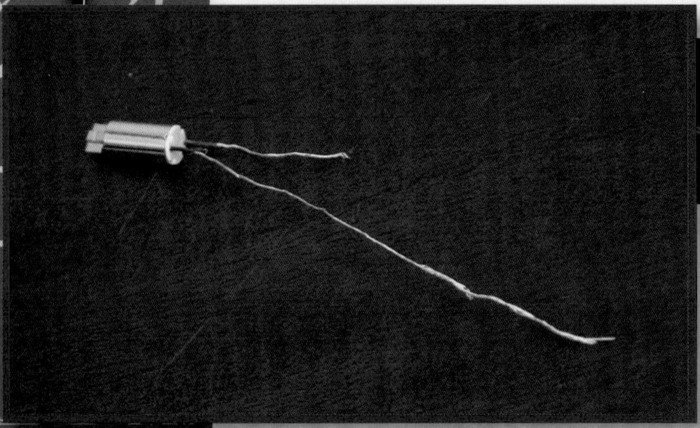

If your motor has wires, strip them. Leave one wire long and cut the other shorter. If your motor has metal prongs, bend one prong underneath the motor and make sure the other prong is sticking up.

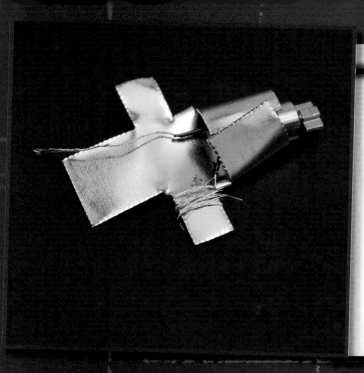

Wrap the end flaps of the tin around the motor to hold it in place. If your motor has wires, wrap the long wire around one of the middle flaps. If your motor has prongs, make sure the one pointing up touches the flaps that hold the motor in place.

Bend up the bottom tab of crafting metal to create a base. Place the battery on the tab. It doesn't matter which side is up. Wrap the middle flaps around the battery to hold it in place.

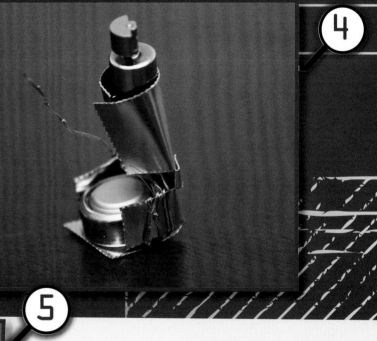

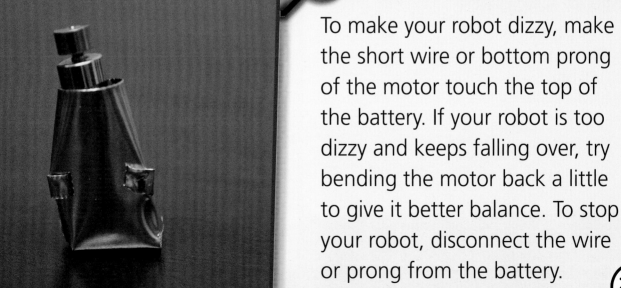

To make your robot dizzy, make the short wire or bottom prong of the motor touch the top of the battery. If your robot is too dizzy and keeps falling over, try bending the motor back a little to give it better balance. To stop your robot, disconnect the wire or prong from the battery.

Build Another Robot

After making a dizzy robot, the RoboBeetle is a great project to try next. You will need an adult to use the hot-glue gun, soldering iron, super glue, and wire cutters for you.

You will need:

- 2 1.5-volt motors
- Holder for 2 AA batteries, with attached wires
- 2 AA batteries
- 2 SPDT switches with levers
- 1 x 3 inch (2.5 x 8 cm) piece of metal
- 2 female quick disconnect terminal connectors
- 22-gauge wire
- Large paper clip
- 4 small paper clips
- Plastic bottle cap
- Wire strippers
- Wire cutters
- Hot-glue gun
- Soldering iron
- Electrical solder
- Epoxy or super glue
- Electrical tape

1

Use the hot-glue gun to attach the SPDT switches to the body of the battery holder. Angle them into an upside-down V shape. Make the prongs under the open ends of the switches touch.

2

Center your piece of metal behind the SPDT switches on the battery holder. Bend down each edge to a 45-degree angle.

3

Tape the motors to the bent pieces of metal so the shafts point down over the edges. Make sure the positive (+) side of one motor lines up with the negative (-) side of the other motor. Use the hot-glue gun to fill the gaps under the tape. Put a ball of hot glue on the end of each shaft.

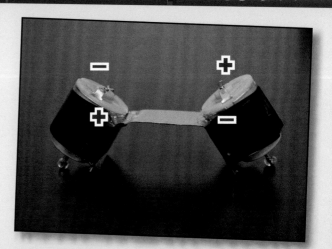

4

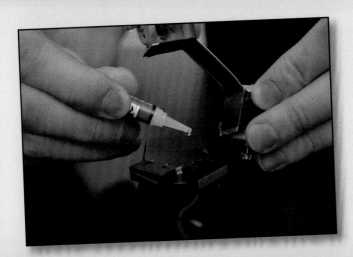

Put strips of electrical tape on the battery holder and the bottom of the metal plate. Put super glue on one of the strips of tape. Glue the two strips together. Put hot glue underneath the metal piece where it bends over the edges of the battery holder.

5

Bend the big paper clip into a Y shape. Use the soldering iron to melt a hole through the plastic cap and put it on the center part of the paper clip. Use lots of hot glue to mount it to the back of the battery holder. This will act as a weight to keep your RoboBeetle from tipping forward.

6

On the SPDT switches, solder together the two prongs that are touching. Unfold a paper clip and cut off a piece long enough to connect the middle prongs of the switches. Unfold another paper clip and cut off pieces long enough to connect the bottom prong of each switch to the top prong of the motor closest to it. Use wire to connect the bottom prongs of the two motors together. Solder all of these connections.

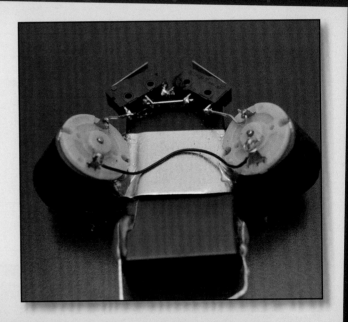

7

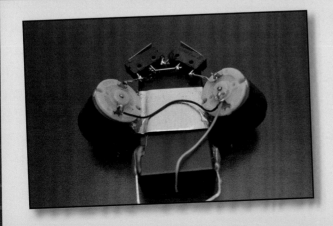

Solder a piece of wire to the negative prong of one motor to a piece of metal at the base of the battery holder. You may need to work the wire inside of the battery holder.

Cut the wires of the battery holder short enough so that they can reach the SPDT switches' prongs. Strip them just a little bit. Solder the red wire to one of the top prongs that are touching. Solder the black wire to one of the middle prongs.

Unfold a small paper clip into an arc. If the connectors have plastic over them, pull it off. Put one end of the unfolded paper clip into the round part of the connector. Pinch it with pliers and then solder it. This is one antenna. Make a second. Slip the clamp ends onto the switches and solder or hot glue them in place.

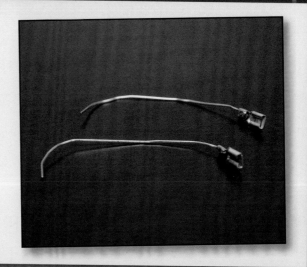

When you put batteries into your RoboBeetle, the motors will start spinning. The balls of hot glue on the motors' shafts will act like tires and make it move. When one of the RoboBeetle's antennae hits something, it will trip an SPDT switch and make one of the motors spin in the reverse direction. This will make the RoboBeetle turn and be able to go around whatever is in its way.

If you don't like how your RoboBeetle looks, you can decorate a plastic lid to make a shell for it. Another fun thing to do with your RoboBeetle is to make an obstacle course for it to go through.

More Robotics Projects

If you liked making a dizzy robot and a robot bug, try making more robots. The following paragraphs mention just a few projects you can find on the Internet. Links to each project can be found in the Projects Links box at the end of this chapter.

Makezine.com has many robotics projects for you to try. One project teaches you how to build a spider robot. Another project uses pool noodles to create the body of a helicopter that you can control or let fly on its own.

Instructables.com is another website where thousands of people post their do-it-yourself (DIY) projects, many of which involve robotics. One project will teach you how to make a little robot that rolls around and explores all on its own.

Some robotics projects need pieces that you can make with a 3D printer. Using 3D printers is another fun way that kids are getting involved in the maker movement.

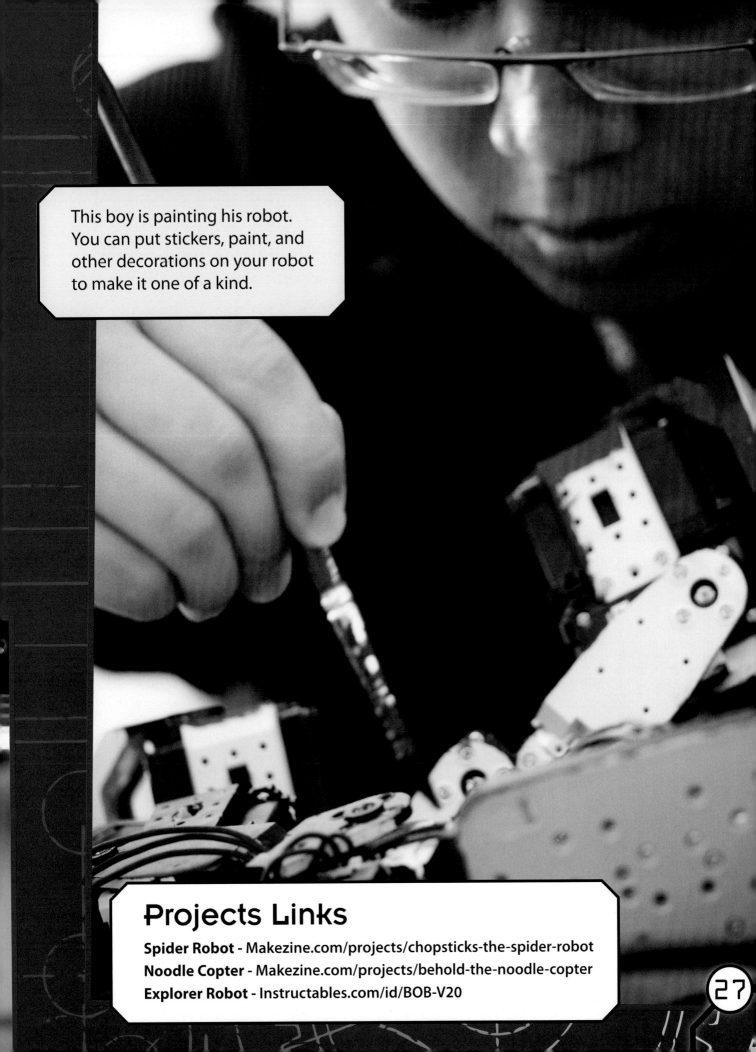

This boy is painting his robot. You can put stickers, paint, and other decorations on your robot to make it one of a kind.

Projects Links

Spider Robot - Makezine.com/projects/chopsticks-the-spider-robot
Noodle Copter - Makezine.com/projects/behold-the-noodle-copter
Explorer Robot - Instructables.com/id/BOB-V20

DIY Is Fun!

Kids all around the world have discovered how fun and easy it is to build robots. The robots you make and program can do all sorts of things. Once you learn the basics, there is no limit to what you can build. After you complete a project, for the next one, try a project that is a little more difficult. You can even change the design and experiment on your own. This is the best way to learn and become better at anything, even building robots.

These students in Palestine have made a robot that will write messages for them.

These boys are working together to build a robot. Working on a project with a friend is a great idea because you can learn from each other.

Robotics is just one part of the maker movement. Once you start making, you will see how fun other high-tech DIY projects are as well. From 3D printing to creating your own musical instruments, there are many ways for you to use your creativity to make something amazing!

Learn More About Making

The list of books, magazines, and websites below can point you in the right direction to learn more about robotics. You can also ask an adult to help you use the library and search the Internet for more projects, books, and places to buy supplies.

Books

Carbaugh, Sam and Kathy Ceceri. *Robotics: Discover the Science and Technology of the Future with 20 Projects*. White River Junction, VT: Nomad Press, 2012.

Malone, Robert. *Recycled Robots: 10 Robot Projects*. New York: Workman Publishing Company, 2012.

Magazines

Make
Robot

Websites

• To find robotics projects to build, go to Letsmakerobots.com.
• There are dozens of videos and tutorials for making robots at Instructables.com.
• For an active online robotics community, take a look at Makezine.com.

High-Tech Parts

Arduino.com
Robotshop.com
Jameco.com
RadioShack stores and Radioshack.com

Glossary

cogs (KAWGZ) Teeth on the rim of a wheel or gear.

complex (kom-PLEKS) Not simple.

fictional (FIK-shnul) Something someone has made up.

programmed (PROH-gramd) Given a set of instructions of when and how to perform an action.

pulleys (PU-leez) Simple machines made up of ropes or chains wrapped around wheels.

robotics (ROW-baw-tiks) Related to designing, building, and using robots.

sensors (SEN-sorz) Devices that gather information.

short-circuit (SHORT-SER-kut) When electricity flows in an unintended way.

solar panels (SOH-ler PA-nulz) Collectors that convert solar energy into electricity.

tutorials (too-TOR-ee-ulz) Lessons.

Index

Websites

Due to the changing nature of Internet links, PowerKids Press has developed an online list of websites related to the subject of this book. This site is updated regularly. Please use this link to access the list: www.powerkidslinks.com/maker/robot/